The Take-away Puppy

Nick was looking
for his brown shoes.
"Here is one," he said.
"Where is the other one?"

Nick's little puppy, Spot,
was under the bed.
He had Nick's other shoe.

"Wuff!" barked Spot.

Spot ran out of the room with the shoe in his mouth.

"Come back with my shoe, Spot!" shouted Nick.

Nick ran after Spot.

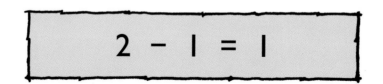

2 – 1 = 1

"You are naughty, Spot,"
laughed Nick.
"That's my shoe.
You are a **take-away puppy.**"

Nick put on his shoes.

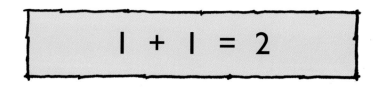

$$1 + 1 = 2$$

On Saturday morning,

Mom and Nick were getting ready

to go shopping.

Mom looked in the box

for their shoes.

"There are three shoes in here,"

she said.

"I can see two of your shoes, Nick,

and one of my shoes.

Where is the fourth shoe?"

$$4 - 1 = 3$$

"Spot, the **take-away puppy**, will have it," said Nick.

Nick went to look in Spot's basket.

"Mom! Here is your shoe!"
shouted Nick.

"Now we have four shoes."

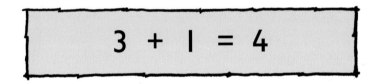

$$3 + 1 = 4$$

In the afternoon, Dad said,

"Let's go to the park.

Here are your shoes, Nick,

and here are Mom's shoes.

Here is one of my shoes,

but where is the other one?"

"Spot will have it," laughed Nick.

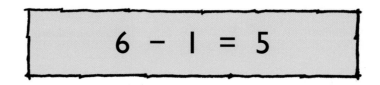

$$6 - 1 = 5$$

Nick went to look for Spot.

He was sitting in his basket

with Dad's shoe.

"Spot," laughed Nick.

"You are a funny **take-away puppy**."

$$5 + 1 = 6$$

$$2 - 1 = 1$$
$$1 + 1 = 2$$

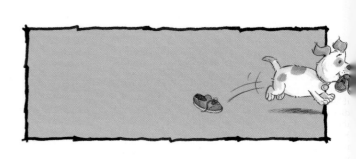

$$4 - 1 = 3$$
$$3 + 1 = 4$$

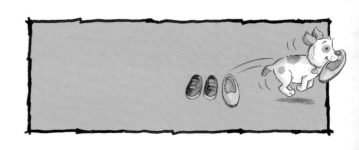

$$6 - 1 = 5$$
$$5 + 1 = 6$$